For Pete
'There's a wideness in God's mercy'
J.D.

For Gerry
A.H.

Text copyright © 2000 Joyce Denham
Illustrations copyright © 2000 Amanda Hall
This edition copyright © 2000 Lion Publishing

The moral rights of the author and illustrator
have been asserted

Published by
Lion Publishing plc
Sandy Lane West, Oxford, England
www.lion-publishing.co.uk
ISBN 0 7459 4503 1 (hardback)
ISBN 0 7459 4523 6 (paperback)
Lion Publishing
4050 Lee Vance View, Colorado Springs,
CO 80918, USA
ISBN 0 7459 4503 1

First UK hardback edition 2000
1 3 5 7 9 10 8 6 4 2 0
First UK paperback edition 2000
1 3 5 7 9 10 8 6 4 2 0
First US edition 2001
1 3 5 7 9 10 8 6 4 2 0

A catalogue record for this book is available
from the British Library

Library of Congress CIP data applied for

Typeset in 15/28 Latin 725 BT
Printed and bound in Malaysia

**This Bible tale is adapted from the story of Jonah,
which can be found in the book of Jonah.**

The Hard to Swallow Tale of

Jonah

and the Whale

Joyce Denham

Illustrated by Amanda Hall

LION
Children's Books

Long ago in the ancient land of the Jews, God spoke to a man named Jonah.

'Get up!' God said. 'Go to the city of Nineveh, and warn the people that their wickedness is about to destroy them.'

Jonah ran to his window and looked east. If he walked for thirty days, he would find Nineveh, that great and glorious city of the Assyrians, sitting on the eastern edge of the world.

But the Assyrians were the enemies of the Jews.

'I would rather die than help those people!' Jonah fumed.

He ran to his other window and looked west, across the sparkling water. If he sailed for many days, he would come to the dirty mining colony of Tarshish, hanging on the western edge of the world.

If I go to Tarshish, Jonah thought, I will be as far from Nineveh as I can get. And I will keep the Lord's love from going to those wicked Assyrians.

But Jonah did not understand that the Lord's compassion had no limits. It stretched all the way across the world—from Tarshish in the west to Nineveh in the east.

So Jonah ran to Joppa, a busy, smelly port on the shore of the Great Sea. There he found a ship where the sailors were loading the last crates of their cargo.

'How far are you sailing?' Jonah called to the captain.

'To the edge of the world!' came the reply.

'To Tarshish.'

'Then let me pay to travel with you,' begged Jonah.

And so it was. The ship set sail that same night.

It was nearly dawn
when a great wind stirred
the waters into a seething rage.
The swells tossed the ship violently.
The sailors cried out to their gods in fear.
'Save us!'
'Don't let us die!'
But the storm blew ever more fiercely.

'We must discover who is responsible for this disaster,' the men agreed. 'We shall cast lots.'

As the winds drew back menacingly, gathering all their might, an eerie calm lingered over the ship. Quickly, everyone put something of his own into a cup, and when the contents were tossed onto the deck, all the pieces fell into a circle.

At the centre was a ring: Jonah's.

The men seized him as the sky split open once again and the sea thundered and crashed.

'Who are you?' they demanded to know. 'Where are you from? Who are your people?'

'I am a Hebrew,' Jonah anxiously explained. 'I worship the Lord, the God of heaven, Maker of sea and land. But I am running away from my God.'

The men gasped in horror.

'What is it you have done to the Lord?' they shouted. 'And what must we do to you to calm the storm?'

'You must throw me into the sea,' Jonah quavered. 'It is my fault that the storm has come upon us.'

'No!' snapped the captain. 'We must row with all our might.'

But it was no use. The storm continued to rage all around them.

The captain knew what he had to do.

'O Lord,' he cried, 'do not judge us for taking this man's life!'

Then they picked up Jonah and threw him over the side of the ship.

He sank beneath the waves and the sea fell calm.

Deep in the cold, dark waters, Jonah's heart froze like stone. Those wicked Assyrians, he thought. Why should they live when I am dying?

But the Lord had prepared a giant fish to swallow Jonah, and to keep him trapped inside until he was ready to listen to the Lord.

It took three days, but in the belly of the fish Jonah's heart warmed. He wondered why he had run from the Lord. And he was so thankful that the Lord had rescued him, he began to sing.

'I cried, Lord, from the raging sea.
You heard my cry! You answered me!

I called, Lord, from the deepest grave.
You heard and you were swift to save!

Your waves and breakers buried me,
Your holy face I could not see.

Dark waters filled my soul with dread,
The seaweed clung about my head.

I sank beneath the mountains' base,
Earth sealed me in at every place.

But you, Lord, raised my soul from death
And from your temple lent me breath.

Why should I flee your holy place
And lose the splendours of your grace?

Salvation comes from God on high—
Maker of earth and sea and sky.

New vows of thanks I ready bring,
O loving Lord, O kindly king!'

Then the Lord commanded the fish to spit Jonah onto
dry land.

'Get up!' God said. 'Now go to the city of Nineveh and warn
those people that their wickedness is about to destroy them!'

Immediately, Jonah got up and did as he was told.

Jonah travelled east for many days before he reached the
splendid gates of Nineveh. He marched through the city, and
at all the crossroads he called out urgently:

'The Lord, the God of heaven, Maker of the sea and land, has
seen your evil. In forty days, all of Nineveh will be destroyed!'

The news spread like fire on a windy day. All over the city,
people heard the alarm.

'If only we had not been so wicked,' they lamented.

They hurried to dress themselves in sackcloth and sat in the
dust to show their remorse—from the very humblest to the

king himself. They called to God for mercy.

And Nineveh was spared.

Jonah was furious.

'O Lord,' he called, 'I knew you would do this. You show mercy to our bitterest enemies. If you let these Assyrians live, I might as well die!'

'Is it right for you to be so angry about the Assyrians?' the Lord asked him.

But Jonah didn't answer. Instead, he ran some way outside the city and built himself a little shelter. Then he folded his arms in anger and sat down to see what would happen to Nineveh next.

So that day, the Lord caused a tall vine to grow next to Jonah's shelter, to protect him from the scorching sun.

And that night, beneath the pleasant, green leaves of the vine, Jonah slept comfortably, still hoping that the Assyrians would perish.

But in the morning, it was the vine that had perished.

'It was such a lovely plant,' Jonah wailed, 'and my only comfort in this barren land.'

'Is it right for you to be so angry about the vine?' God asked him.

'Yes it is,' snarled Jonah. 'I'm so angry I want to die!'

Then God spoke to him one more time.

'O Jonah,' God said, 'if you are so troubled over the loss of a vine, think of what I feel for Nineveh—its people and its animals.'

Jonah was silent.

Before him towered the gates of the city—a city full of sheep and cattle and 120,000 Assyrians whose lives had been saved.

Then he took down his shelter and headed home.

At last he understood that the Lord's compassion had no limits. It reached from the heights of heaven to the depths of the dark, angry sea; and it stretched all the way across the world—from Tarshish in the west to Nineveh in the east.